MW01716180

Living As God's Beloved

Meeting The Secular And Surviving

WALTER H. KREBS

Fairway Press
Lima, Ohio

LIVING AS GOD'S BELOVED

FIRST EDITION

ISBN 0-7880-0656-8 PRINTED IN U.S.A.

Dedicated to —

my good friends at Evangelical United Church of Christ, Godfrey, Illinois,

and

Fr. Henri Nouwen for his gift of grace to us who learn to know the Spirit through him.

Table Of Contents

Preface

None of us creates out of a vacuum. There are always those who have *gone before*.

There are also those contemporaries who *light the way*, not only by the depth of their insight but also by their charisma.

Such a man is Father Henri Nouwen! Father Nouwen, a Dutch priest, formerly of the faculties of Notre Dame, Yale and Harvard, is now pastor of **Daybreak**, a Canadian L'Arche community for the mentally impaired.

It was my good fortune to attend the United Church Of Christ Annual Pastors Consultation in Orlando, Florida, in January of 1992 where Father Nouwen was the featured speaker. It was for all who heard him an experience in Christian charisma! We were moved! We were changed!

This book of sermons grew out of that experience. Building on Henri Nouwen's variety of insights concerning the struggle to live as God's People in a secular society, I endeavored to *bring the message home* as a Lenten/Easter series for the good people of Evangelical United Church Of Christ, Godfrey, Illinois, whom it was my privilege to serve as pastor for 24 years. Their response was enthusiastic! It was also encouraging regarding publication. Hence, this effort.

I was also encouraged in this effort by a letter from Henri Nouwen with whom I shared my manuscript. Father Nouwen wrote: "I am very happy that in this way my presentations in Florida have continuing impact. . . Thanks so much for making me part of your ministry."

So I dedicate these sermons to my good friends at Evangelical Church, with special thanks to Henri Nouwen for his gift of Christian grace to all of us who sat at his feet at the Florida Pastors Consultation.

Thanks, too, to Barbara Green, my former secretary, who had to struggle with hand-written manuscripts in order to prepare typed copies, first for the pulpit, then for publication.

All scriptural references and quotations are from The New English Bible unless otherwise noted. Other quotations are footnoted.

Pastor Walter H. Krebs

Godfrey, Illinois
September 10, 1995

Introduction

Never Far From Home

Psalm 51:1-4, 10-12; 2 Corinthians 5:20b—6:2; Luke 15:11-32

There are two familiar biblical texts which clearly define our Lord's divine nature. Both include a heavenly voice which validates both his person and his ministry. As you may recall, one was heard at his baptism and the other on the Mount of Transfiguration. You know the words: "This is my Beloved Son on whom my favor rests. Listen to him!"

And what does Jesus tell us? He tells us that we, too, are beloved sons and daughters of God. He tells us that even when we wander away from home, even when we do not act as sons and daughters, still we are never far from home. The accent is always on home-coming. Indeed, the accent of the whole of scripture is upon such reconciliation. It is not upon fear and damnation as so many of the fundamentalists would have us believe!

It was the great seventeenth century artist, Rembrandt, who gave us that splendid painting of the parable of the Prodigal Son which portrays the heart of God's redemptive plan so beautifully. In that painting, as the well-known prodigal master of wine, women, and song returns home, after having wasted his inheritance in riotous living, Rembrandt pictures him kneeling before his father who, literally, enfolds him with his billowing, bright red robes.

Do you get the picture? The boy comes home, hat in hand, prepared to grovel before his father, anticipating the worst. But what does his father do? He enfolds him with love! He says, symbolically, as he surrounds him with the folds of his robes, "You are never far from home because you are always in my heart." Then he throws a wild celebration to welcome the return of his beloved son.

Do you get the picture? When we find our true home within the folds of God's loving embrace, we are at once freed of our anxiety over our imperfections and our foolishnesses so that we can become what God wants us to become.

II

That is best understood, I think, when we examine the life of the elder brother. To the naked eye, he was the perfect son. He obeyed his dad's every wish. He probably even tried to anticipate the old man's wishes in order to impress him. In Old Testament terms, he tried to obey every jot and tittle of the law. He tried to prove himself worthy of his dad's love. He would never have asked for his inheritance in advance, much less squandered it on wild living. To the naked eye, the elder brother was as perfect a son as one could be.

But what was behind his goodness came out in his hostility against the return of his younger brother. He didn't understand how parental love works. He didn't know about its *enfolding* nature: how it grieves when wrong is done, and how it longs to welcome back the erring son or daughter.

My reading of this story is that the elder brother was literally afraid to *try his wings* because he feared that if he *blew it*, he would not be able to go back home again, either because he was too proud, or because his father would not take him back, or both!

It all reminds me of the elderly woman, a very pious, good soul, well known in her church, who once said to me, "If it weren't for the fear of hell, I'd really live it up!"

Well, whatever else that suggests, it certainly does not suggest spiritual freedom, born of God's love, whose last word, even in the face of our sin, is always: "You are my beloved son or daughter; you are never out of my heart. You are never far from home!"

And isn't that what God's work of redemption in Jesus Christ is all about? It is the dramatic example of our chosenness by God, who welcomes us home even when we have gone off and done something stupid!

Rembrandt's painting of the father's grand embrace is the most powerful symbol I know as we try to understand, and take to ourselves, the fact that, like Jesus, we too are God's beloved!

III

In this series of sermons I will be talking about some specific approaches by which we can make God's all-enfolding love a part of our consciousness. I will be talking about those practical, simple, everyday, spiritual disciplines whereby we can learn to live in the freedom with which the Prodigal Son lived his life: free to make mistakes; free to trust in God's forgiving love; free to come home again to the safety of love till we find the courage to try again; free, despite the world's temptations, to pursue its countless opportunities; free, as God's beloved sons and daughters, to pursue, without fear of error, Christ's work of truth, of justice, of peace, of goodness, in a sin-sick world; free, because we are never far from home.

In that spirit, I enfold you in his name!

Staying In Touch

Psalm 91:1-2, 9-16 (KJV); Romans 10:8b-13; Luke 4:1-13

This is the beginning of a series of sermons devoted to the development of some personal spiritual disciplines in behalf of the God-centered life.

Now, at once, that is a frightening thought! It sounds like an invitation to prolonged periods of inactivity centered in religious exercises.

Such fear is understandable! For we live in a world that has taught us not to tolerate inactivity, to despise non-productivity. In the words of the Dutch philosopher, Spinoza, "We fear the empty place." Therefore, we do everything possible to stay occupied.

Have you ever heard a teenager contemplate a Friday or Saturday night when *nothing's going on*? There is literally panic in the voice because teenagers can't stand inactivity any more than we can! Indeed, if I were to suggest that for the next 30 minutes all of us sit perfectly still and meditate, we'd go crazy! In Henri Nouwen's descriptive phrase, "We'd end up behaving like a bunch of hungry monkeys in a banana tree." We can't stand inactivity!

So it is that the word *discipline* has become as negative to the adult mind as it is in the minds of our kids, for whom discipline is only seen in terms of punishment or something distasteful, like practicing a musical instrument or doing homework.

But as I point out to my confirmation classes, *discipline* also has a different meaning. It comes from the same word from which *disciple* comes, and that means *one who follows.* In Christian terms, spiritual discipline means to pattern our life after our Lord in a purposeful way; to adopt certain disciplines whereby we are helped to succeed in our goal of being Jesus' disciple.

I

I want now to talk about the discipline of prayer. I want to talk about prayer as *staying in touch with God* in such a way that we allow God to mold our living as Jesus did.

But more than that, I want to talk about prayer, not so much in terms of stopping everything we're doing in order to say some pious words, but as creating an open space in our inner self in which God can speak to us and guide our living.

That, incidentally, is the function of preaching and the Sunday liturgy. These functions of worship try to create in the midst of the worshipping congregation spaces in which God can speak to us.

You know that by experience! How often, during a sermon, do you find yourself going off in a direction of thought all your own because of something I have said, even though it may not be connected to the main point of the sermon? Indeed, by the time you get back to what I am saying I may be nearly finished. Yet, in the time in-between, God has spoken to you.

The same thing may be said about the prayers, the lessons, or even the verses of a hymn. Often a verse of scripture, a prayer-thought, or a hymn-verse may take you away from what the rest of us are saying, or doing, on your own spiritual journey. Has it ever occurred to you that at such points a window is being opened to your inner being through which the spirit of God may enter to speak with you? Praying is not always saying things, or doing things, by form or habit. It is more than that! To pray is also to create an open space in which God can speak and guide your thoughts and desires.

II

I like Henri Nouwen's definition of prayer. He says it this way:

> *To pray does not mean only to think about God in contrast to thinking about other things, or to spend time with God instead of spending time with other people. Prayer also means to think and live in the presence of God. It means to move ourselves away from a self-centered monologue to a God-centered dialogue as did our Lord during his days of temptation.*[1]

Such is Henri Nouwen's response to St. Paul's dictum that "We should pray without ceasing" (1 Thessalonians 5:17-18).

But realizing the speed with which we live, Father Nouwen converts our *banana tree* mentality to a new approach to the constancy of prayer. "How," he asks, "can we turn our ceaseless activity into praying? How can our thinking, in the midst of our many activities, become a time of prayer for us without stopping what we're doing?"

Well, it depends upon to whom, or to what, we direct our thoughts! For thinking is an on-going process from morning till night. It covers the gamut from what we're going to wear, to our schedule for the day, to things we're happy about, to things we worry about, to with whom, if anyone, we feel free to share our innermost thoughts and needs.

Thinking goes on all the time, even at night in our dreams. So it is that psychiatrists Sigmund Freud and Carl Jung tell us that even our dreams may reveal great truths about us. Therefore, the question remains, "Toward whom, or toward what, do we direct our thinking?"

That means praying is more than saying pious words while kneeling at the bedside or sitting in the church sanctuary. For to pray ceaselessly, as St. Paul directs, is constantly to process our thoughts, and our feelings, according to our faith in God. Such praying means that we invite God into our lives in their every dimension. It means prayerfully thinking through such simple questions as these:

- Does God smile on the goals in life I have adopted?
- Does God smile on my use of time and energy?
- Have I made God my companion and friend?
- What might God suggest I do about the things I'm worried about today?
- Am I open to God's influence in my thoughts and actions or have I already made up my mind?

To stay in touch with God does not imply ceaseless formal religious activity. It means that we constantly hold those major thoughts and feelings, which are so much a part of us, up to God. In other words, thinking can become praying if we want it to. It can become that means of living in the presence of God whereby we listen to what is being said to us before we act.

III

But there is more! Such listening helps to create obedience! Indeed, in Latin, the verb *listen* is a derivative of the word *obey*. That means that to live as God's beloved involves obedient listening to what God has to say. And that's the kind of prayer we're talking about. It is that reflective thinking which creates a space for God within so that we may be led by his light and truth.

By way of contrast, our English word *deaf* is related to the Latin words for *absurd*. It describes those who no longer listen to the *Words of Life*. It suggests those for whom all sorts of addictions — money, sex, power, alcohol, drugs, or whatever — have become absurd substitutes which deafen them to the love of God.

So it is that ceaseless praying, by which we submit our ongoing thoughts and feelings to the indwelling spirit of God for review, becomes for us a spiritual discipline. It becomes an act of obedience by which we stay constantly in touch with God. It is a way of creating for God that means of contact by which we can shape our living as his beloved son or daughter.

IV

Let me offer, then, some simple suggestions whereby you may begin the process of praying through reflective thinking.

First, establish firmly in your consciousness that you are, indeed, God's beloved. How? By memorizing these lines from Psalm 131:

> *My heart is not proud, I do not set my sights too high;*
> *No, I hold myself in silence (before God) like a child in its mother's arms.*

Memorize those lines. Say them over and over again each day — as often as you have opportunity — until they become part of you. Keep them at the top of your consciousness so that they become like a window through which you look at your life. For only as you discipline your life by exercising the Divine Presence can you live as God's beloved.

Second, select a few verses of scripture to memorize for practical use when you need them.

If you're the worrying type, memorize our Lord's words: "Be not concerned for tomorrow. Let tomorrow take care of itself" (Matthew 6:34). Worry doesn't change anything anyway!

If you are the impatient type, memorize Isaiah's words: "In quietness shall be your strength" (Isaiah 30:15). Among other things, it may help you get through the checkout line at the supermarket!

If you are the *hot-headed, fly-off-the-handle* type, memorize the proverb: "A soft answer turns away anger" (Proverbs 15:1). It may save you from a lost friendship or even a bloody nose!

If you are the nervous type, memorize the words: "Be still and know that I am God" (Psalm 46:10). It may prevent you from driving yourself and your family crazy.

If you lack generosity, memorize the words: "God loves a cheerful giver" (II Corinthians 9:7). It may save you from a shriveled-up soul.

If you are overly-concerned about the material things of life, memorize our Lord's words: "What will it profit you to gain the whole world at the expense of your soul?" (Matthew 16:26). It may lead you to a broader, more meaningful view of life.

These are simply examples of the kinds of prayer-thoughts by which we can direct our living as God's beloved people.

But that takes discipline! So we end where we began. To be a disciple of Jesus is to discipline our thinking through prayer-thoughts as we do our living each day. For prayer is not only withdrawal to the sanctuary or bedside. Prayer is also staying in touch with God in the common ventures of life. In the words of Henri Nouwen:

> *When we give prayer serious attention and develop an appropriate discipline, we will see a real transformation in our lives — a transformation that will lead us closer and closer to God. Then we will realize that prayer is the constant practice of the presence of God at all times and in all places.*[2]

---

1. Henri Nouwen, *Clowning In Rome*, (New York: Bantam Doubleday Dell, 1979), pp. 70-71.

2. *Ibid.* p. 83.

Avoiding Inner Clutter

Psalm 24:1-7; Philippians 3:17-20; 4:8-9; John 7:37-46

In the last chapter I talked about prayer as something more than pious activity in the church or at the bedside. I spoke of prayer as a matter of thinking: a matter of thinking about how we are dealing with the daily experiences of life against the background of our faith. I spoke about *prayer-thoughts*. For in that kind of praying we create a space for God at the very heart of our being into which God can enter and help us deal with the whole gamut of life's experiences: its joys, sorrows, loves, angers, confidences, fears, certainties, and confusions. Such praying keeps us constantly in touch with God because such praying is not centered in little islands of withdrawal from life. No! Thinking-prayers are centered in what we are feeling and doing at the moment. That's what ceaseless, practical prayer is all about. It's a matter of reflecting together with God on our life-activities and experiences as they are happening.

But, in order to do such praying, it is necessary to provide space for it. That means it is necessary to slow down and to avoid that inner clutter which so fills our brain and our emotions that there is little room for God.

I

First, the matter of slowing down.

Picture it! The time is 7:30 a.m., Monday through Friday. My neighbor's garage door flies up, the car shoots out of the garage, the door automatically closes, and the horn begins to toot loudly and impatiently. If the weather is warm so that the car window can stand open, the mother also shouts, "Get out here!" The kids amble out, climb into the car, and the car roars up the street toward school. What a way to start the day!

Another neighbor used to rush out of the house each morning with his coffee cup, hell-bound for work. "My goodness," I used to think, "he's really the executive type." Only later did I learn that the coffee cup contained vodka. That was the way his day started. He has since died of a bad liver.

Some time ago a teenager told me that his parent uses the daily ride to the high school, on the parent's way to work, as the opportunity to *harp* at him about *whatever.* What a way to start the day!

Does it ever occur to us that we set ourselves up for frustration, anger, disappointment, poor family relationships, and poor job performance simply by the way we start the day? We're so busy getting ready to *run and do* that there is no time to nourish our spirit or the spirits of those whom we love. The clutter of the mind — the assault on the mind by the pressures we allow to overcome us — is often our undoing!

Slowing down so that we can have our prayer-thoughts is an important spiritual discipline. It is spiritually healthy to take a leisurely shower, and, as the warm water caresses your body, to think, "This is the day the Lord has made; I will rejoice and be glad in it." There is spiritual health in a simple breakfast with loved ones whereby, instead of storming around to get away to school or to the job, we leave feeling loved and appreciated. There's spiritual health in arriving ten minutes early at school, or the job, for a short time of friendly interaction before the tasks begin. That's why I've always asked my classes to arrive early.

Why do I call these things spiritual disciplines? They are spiritual disciplines because they set the tone for how we face the day. They create the time and the space for those prayer-thoughts by which we prepare ourselves to face, perhaps, a difficult task or a disagreeable person. They create the time for that patience and understanding which all harmonious human interaction requires. And they allow us to deal with whatever our own inner needs may be at the moment.

The psalmist asks us today, "Who may go up the mount of the Lord? Who may stand in God's holy place?" And the answer? "Those with clean hands and a pure heart; who have not set their minds on falsehood."

At this point, I read the word *falsehood* not only to mean the dishonesties of life, but also the habit of so many people who let their lives be governed by the non-spiritual: by that rushed, harsh, self-centered, undisciplined living which approaches even God aggressively, demanding whatever we have set our minds to. That is the spiritual falsehood which makes us unfit to stand in God's holy place.

To live as God's beloved it becomes necessary to create the time and the space in which to do it, even if that requires a major adjustment in our time-schedule. In a word, we first have to slow down in order to make room for godliness to happen.

II

But there is another dimension to all of this. It has to do with avoiding that inner clutter created, in general, by the world. I don't know much about computers. But I do know one of that technology's standard slogans regarding computer use. It says, "Garbage in, garbage out." What you put into the machine is what you get out!

I think that's also a good slogan insofar as our senses are concerned, for it raises the question: "What do you allow in?"

Take, for instance, the news media. In Henri Nouwen's words, "We cling to the news of the day as if we could control it." Well, of course, we can't! Yet we read and watch, with fascination, reports of rapes and murders, of terrible accidents, of drug busts, of crime and corruption, as if our very life depended upon it. "Why not," asks Father Nouwen, "catch up on the news once a week? You can't do anything about it, anyway!"

Or take the matter of the television talk shows — "freak shows," as I heard one person refer to them. One tries to outdo the other in presenting the world's craziness for public consumption! It is only made worse by the audience reaction, with its mostly ignorant comments.

I think Father Nouwen is right when he says that the images of life projected by television, both in its news reporting and in its programming, are not good for us. For they clutter up our *innards* with the perverse in life.

Recently the American Psychological Association declared that "watching TV can lead to anti-social behavior, obesity, gender and racial stereotyping, bad grades, and a lack of self-esteem for families."

It went on to report that the average child watches 8,000 murders and 100,000 other acts of violence by the time he or she leaves elementary school. The Association then goes on to say: "There is extensive evidence that TV violence can influence aggressive attitudes and behavior." Beyond all of that, the report suggests that "families may come to feel inadequate when they compare themselves to the affluent, successful families that predominate prime-time programs."[1]

Now these are not *off the cuff* pronouncements. For the 195 page report, from which these quotes are taken, is the result of five years of research by the American Psychological Association's Task Force on Television and Society.

Those television images, projected both in programming and commercials, are literally seductive! For they create within us wants and desires. They generate feelings and attitudes. They teach values and life-outlooks which cater to the most crass and most base of human attitudes and emotions.

All of which is to say that while our kind of media may have not existed during New Testament times, the problem back then in the Greek culture was the same. Therefore, the epistle lesson continues to be applicable as St. Paul says to us:

Whatever is true, whatever is honorable, whatever is just, whatever is pure, whatever is lovely, whatever is gracious, if there is any excellence, if there is anything worthy of praise, think about these things . . . and the God of peace will be with you!

III

To avoid inner clutter, to avoid the damaging of our spirits, whether by the perverse as depicted on television and reported by the media, or by the loss of control over our daily schedules, requires discipline. What is needed is a spiritual discipline which creates a space within our hearts and minds for God, a space in which God can speak in the silence of our thoughts, whether in the shower, in the car on the way to work, in school, or in a mental *time out* in the midst of what we are doing.

To control our senses in order to avoid inner clutter is to lay the groundwork for those prayer-thoughts which keep our lives on track, thoughts like today's gospel in which our Lord invites us to drink of "the streams of living water which flow out of him."

---

1. *Big World, Small Screen*, ed. Aletha C. Huston, University Of Nebraska Press, Lincoln, Nebraska, 1992. Used by permission of the publisher.

Meaningful Routines

Psalm 19:7-14; Philippians 2:1-4, 14-16; Matthew 25:14-30 (RSV)

The overall goal of this series of sermons is to offer some helps as to how we can live as God's beloved.

We began with some thoughts as to how the very same words spoken over Jesus at his baptism, and, again, at his transfiguration, belong to us — those words from heaven which announced, "This is my beloved Son." We are, indeed, God's beloved sons and daughters!

But in order to live our lives in that mode we need to stay in touch with the God who loves us. So we spoke of prayer as the means of doing that. We talked of praying, not so much in terms of withdrawing to the silence of the sanctuary or to the privacy of our bedside. We spoke, instead, about prayer-thoughts. We spoke about doing our daily activities prayerfully. How? By holding up to God, in reflection, our purposes, our attitudes, our feelings, our ways of dealing with the many questions and activities in which we are engaged. We do it by asking ourselves such questions as these: Do I feel thankful for the good things that come my way? What is the Christian way of handling this or that difficult situation? Do I filter my living through the teachings of my faith? Those are really all prayer-thoughts! They are thoughts which give Christian direction to our lives so that we are able to live as God's beloved.

But in order to do that we need to make room for prayer-thoughts by avoiding inner clutter, by putting a *governor* on what we allow to enter our thoughts and feelings. We need to censor, among other things, the impact of television and the rest of the media upon us. We need to train our minds to filter out the unwholesome so that there is room for the good, the true, the beautiful and the uplifting.

All of which is to say that we need to develop patterns of spiritual discipline in our living.

I want to illustrate how that can work to our advantage in our approach to the routines of life.

I

Now, at once, this becomes a difficult task, for *routine* suggests repetition, and repetition suggests boredom.

Sticking mailing labels on the weekly church paper can be boring. Cleaning the floors in the church fellowship hall, not once, but several times a day after the various classes have eaten there, can be boring. Doing the weekly housework or yardwork can be boring. Doing repetitive classwork or homework in order to master a subject can be boring. *Working out*, athletically or on a musical instrument, in order to be good, can be boring.

Life is full of routines! So the question is not: Routines versus no routines. No, the question is: "Can we make those routines meaningful?"

Well, that depends entirely upon the spirit in which we approach them.

II

Henri Nouwen, to whom I am deeply indebted for many of the thoughts in these sermons, taught me a new way of looking at life's routines.

Father Nouwen's ministry, after years of being a distinguished university professor and author, is now to a Canadian community of mentally impaired people. The level of impairment extends from the profoundly retarded, who need complete care, to the mildly so, who are able to assist in taking care of the needs of their fellow-residents.

Several of these residents were present at the 1992 United Church Of Christ Annual Pastors Consultation which I attended, and which featured Father Nouwen as guest lecturer. In their presentations these men spoke of how they deal with the potential boredom in their daily routines, which include dressing, feeding, even diapering some of the more difficult residents, as well as doing the mundane chores of laundry, washing dishes, cleaning, and guiding the recreation of the more capable residents. "Boredom," they said, "is an ever-present temptation." To suggest otherwise would be naive, even dishonest! Yet in thinking of their work as a ministry to those less fortunate than themselves they find a positive response to the temptation to boredom.

Having visited such a community during my seminary days, I would say that those who find meaning in such a ministry are truly echoes of St. Paul's words in the epistle lesson: "They shine like stars in a dark world, offering a word of life."

Well, that's a dramatic way of finding meaning in the routines of life. Yet, we can do the same thing!

I can still remember my mother's ironing routine after she had to go back to work. The ironing board would be set up in the dining room, usually on Tuesday evening, so that she could interact with us kids who were gathered in the adjacent living room doing homework or listening to the radio — to The Lone Ranger or some such program. Over the course of several hours she might iron a dozen or more starched shirts — a wearisome task! But she always said that she liked her men to look good, and that gave her work meaning.

That same mind-set is characteristic of dedicated teachers. At the beginning of a new school year we may think, "O God! Here we go again!" But soon such thoughts are replaced by the needs and challenges of a new batch of students so that routine lesson plans become meaningful experiences as we try to communicate them to the students.

Or take the matter of preparing for the celebration of the eucharist, especially if it is to be served in the pews. The filling and, later, washing of hundreds of little wine glasses is a tedious task. Some hate it! Yet others feel that it is a high privilege to be stewards of the sacrament, and so they find meaning in attending to these chores in behalf of Christ's eucharist for his beloved people.

After 39 years of ministry I can truthfully say that I still find meaning in the many liturgical details I must attend to in preparation for services.

The same can be said about many of those in the public service industry.

Some years ago I had to go to Chicago to conduct the funeral service of a family member. It was December, the weather was threatening, and the time schedule was tight. So my wife and I decided to take the train. Well, the train was four hours late, we were highly agitated, and, to make matters worse, no cab driver wanted to drive as far as we had to travel from the train station. But, finally, we found a driver who would. He soon sensed our frustration as we began to tell our tale of woe. At that point he said, "Now you just sit back and relax. I'm going to get you home. It won't be long. Everything will be okay." That from a cab driver who, undoubtedly, missed several fares by accepting one long trip on a cold, wet, wintery night in Chicago!

Friends, that was a ministry on his part which, I'm sure, he did for others as well, and which gave meaning to the routine of a cab driver's life.

III

In the gospel we heard our Lord's familiar parable of how three men used their talents in dealing with their master's money. Now, at this point, the preacher usually tells us that not everyone has the same talent, or even the same amount of talent, but that each of us is expected to capitalize on whatever talent we may have. That, of course, is true.

But have you ever felt any sympathy for the guy in this story who received only two bags of gold? He didn't have nearly as much to work with as did the other two who received the ten bags and the five bags. In other words, his resources were limited!

Now when you translate that into talents, the emphasis is still on limited resources. This guy was not highly gifted! He was just an average Joe whose life centered mainly in the routines of home life, of doing his job — maybe driving a cab — and in his leisure time, of doing average things.

No problem with that! But where he got into trouble was that he did not even use the opportunities which came his way. That's how he lost everything. In today's context, that's where he sank into boredom rather than finding meaning in the routines of his life.

IV

Back in 1948, Elton Trueblood, professor of philosophy at Earlham College, a Quaker school, wrote an important little book titled, *The Common Ventures Of Life.* In that book Professor Trueblood dealt with the question of the sacred possibilities contained in the common, routine ventures of life. Let me quote an important observation of his:

> *In our modern world millions find it hard to know how to dignify their lives. Most cannot. . . do anything on a grand scale. So they feel like bees in a hive rather than as free (people) able to exercise voluntary choice in determining the nature of their contributions to mankind.*
>
> *We cannot change all of this in a moment. But the best way to begin to change it is to recover the largely lost sense that work ought to be sacred. It ought to be a window through which the divine light can shine.*[1]

But it is up to us to find that light, to find meaning in the routines of our living. How? I think our Lord would say, "By living as God's beloved," by regarding our routines as a form of prayer, as a form of spiritual endeavor, lifted up to God.

To that end let me propose this personal inventory. Review in your mind the routines of your life and ask yourself, "How may I use those routines — "

- for the upbuilding of my faith?
- for the upbuilding of my family?
- for the upbuilding of my church?
- for the blessing of those I meet and work with?
- for the benefit of my community?

In other words, how can I make my routines meaningful?

In the early years of my ministry a 19-year-old boy in my first parish became schizophrenic. He was totally *out of it* and had to be hospitalized. He was there for six months. They didn't know much about treating schizophrenia in those days so there was some doubt as to his recovery. I visited him twice weekly, week in and week out. I conferred regularly with the psychiatrist. I did everything I could think of to help. But nothing seemed to do any good, and I feared that Lester would be lost to us forever.

One day when I arrived for my visit Lester was lying on his bed holding a jelly cookie, which a volunteer had placed in his hand, staring at his jelly-smeared, sticky fingers. He paid little attention to me until I wet my handkerchief at the sink, took the cookie from him, and washed his hand. At that point he turned, looked at me, smiled, and said: "You're nice!" That was his first really appropriate response in months. Some weeks later he was ready to receive Holy Communion. Then, not too long after that, I was able to pick him up from the hospital and take him home. Some years later we were invited to his wedding.

I like to think that God used that routine washing of the jelly from Lester's hand to help bring him back.

Routines can be boring, or they can be made meaningful, depending upon how you look at them, and the use you make of them. It's up to us as God's beloved people to uncover the difference!

---

1. Elton Trueblood, *The Common Ventures Of Life*, (New York: Harper, 1949), pp. 102-103.

Keeping A Clear Head

Psalm 119:105-112; 1 Timothy 6:17-21; Matthew 6:24-34

In this series of sermons we have been saying that living as God's beloved requires that we stay in touch with God through that kind of prayer-thinking in which we pass before God's eyes our thoughts, our feelings, and our intended actions while they are still happening, in order to ask whether God approves.

In addition, we have said that it is important to censor what we allow into our thoughts and feelings — those images of life which are unwholesome and destructive of spirituality. We need to avoid the *inner clutter* of so much that comes our way through the media, through the entertainment industry, and through the *junk* of life about which we can't do a thing.

Then we talked about the routines of life and how we can find spiritual meaning in them. We talked about how those routines can become our ministry: our contribution of love toward family, toward friends, toward our work-associates, and even toward the stranger.

Now, obviously, all of these things require discipline, and that's not a popular word with most of us. But may I remind you, please, that the word *discipline* is related to the word *disciple*. Therefore, if we are truly intent on living as God's beloved, as disciples of his Son, it then becomes necessary that we accept certain disciplines in behalf of that intention.

I want to talk about the discipline of spiritual reading and study, for the sake of our growth in discipleship and spirituality.

I

The great concert pianist Paderewski, of a generation ago — he was also president of Poland — used to say:

> *If I do not practice for a day, I know it. If I do not practice for two days, the critics know it. If I do not practice for three days, the audience knows it.*

That is a good analogy for our spirituality. What we believe about God is not enough! In order to keep our Christian perspective alive we need to keep practicing the presence of God through reading and study.

That's what lies behind today's Psalm reading. The writer looks at all of the negatives in his own life, and in his world, and he prays: "I am cruelly afflicted, O Lord. Revive me!"

And then he goes on to say: "Thy instruction is my everlasting inheritance. It is the joy of my heart! Every day, when I take my life into my hands, I never forget."

And what does he never forget? He never forgets that "God's Word is a lamp to guide his feet and a light on his path." Why? Because it is that Word which leads to communion with God.

Some years ago now, Buckingham Palace announced that the marriage between Fergie and Prince Andrew was *kaput.* Why? Because Andrew was gone so much of the time that they became strangers. Indeed, they became such strangers that there was nothing left to revive.

I think that is the way it is for many Christians. There's nothing wrong with their beliefs. It's just that they and God are strangers. There is no familiarity, no warmth, no inner experience that God is real, that God is more than a theological abstraction about whom the church talks in her creeds and statements of faith.

With the psalmist, with the prophets, with the disciples, with the mystics, all of whom center their lives in communion with a real, living, available, personal God, it is different! For them, and for many ordinary people like them, the words of the psalmist are ever so true: "Every day, when I take my life into my hands (to do whatever the day requires), I never forget thy instruction."

But for that to be true we have to read regularly about God. For if it is true that the Spirit speaks to us through God's Word — that scripture is a Holy Light — then we need to be students of that Word in order to hear the voice of God.

We have, also, to read the writings of people like Henri Nouwen, and other teachers in the field of spirituality, in order that God may become our companion. For without that ongoing companionship the very thing we need most — a daily communing with God, in the midst of our activities — will be missing.

II

All of which is to say that it is not enough to filter out those negative forces of life which clutter our minds and emotions with their negative effects. We need, also, to put ourselves in touch with those positive things that help us keep a clear head!

Yet, just how confused many people are in terms of what it means to live with clear-headed faith was revealed in a recent Library of Congress survey. The survey asked people to name what book has been most influential in their lives. Well, as one might expect, the Bible ranked number one. The number two book, however, was Ayn Rand's *Atlas Shrugged*, a book which glorifies extreme individualism, scorns concern for the welfare of others, and promotes what Rand calls rational self-interest.

Now that's quite a contradiction! And the only logical explanation I can think of for those who claim scripture to be the primary influence in their lives, and then embrace such contradictory views as expressed by Ayn Rand, is that they look at scripture not so much as the means for communion with God. They regard scripture simply as the repository of religiously-oriented, self-serving, wise sayings; sayings like those pithy little snippets for which the *Reader's Digest* is famous; sayings which suggest that we can control our own lives, using God in the process.

Perhaps that's the point of the epistle lesson in which St. Paul writes to Timothy:

> *Teach those who are steeped in this world's goods (including its self-centered philosophy) not to be so proud, not to fix their hopes on these uncertain things. But to fix their hopes upon God who can endow us richly with all things to enjoy.*

Paul then goes on to say:

> *Tell them to turn a deaf ear to empty worldly chatter, and to the contradictions of so-called knowledge, for many who have laid claim to such knowledge have shot far wide of the faith.*

All of which is to say that we need clear heads to live as God's beloved, and that takes the kind of disciplined study and spiritual insight of which the psalm speaks. It takes the governing of one's life, daily, by the Light of God which comes to us through scripture and through the other great teachers of the faith.

III

Finally, in order to keep a clear head we need to guard against practicing our religion backwards.

Henri Nouwen makes a convincing point when he tells us not to start out with the *issues* of life, with either our personal struggles or the great social struggles of peace, poverty, prejudice, the AIDS epidemic, the pollution of the environment, the problems of education or whatever. For when we start out with such issues we exhaust ourselves so that we become frustrated, we become angry, we become argumentative, and we become *scolding moralists*, always wanting to tell others how wrong they are.

Let me give you an example. In a pastor's convention I attended there appeared a speaker well known for his radical social stands, and for his issue-centered approach to the gospel. Well, by the time the sermon was finished most of were mad as hell. His verbal brick bats, his arrogance, and his moral self-righteousness, accomplished nothing. That, incidentally, is a lesson which many denominational leaders need to learn!

By way of contrast, Henri Nouwen's talks were spiritually upbuilding. They brought us into the presence of God! And when he mentioned the poor, the homeless, the AIDS-afflicted, together with those destructive *isms* which afflict our society, we heard God saying to us through Henri Nouwen: "Friends, this ought not to be!" We heard our Lord saying: "Whatever you do for the afflicted, you do for me." As a result, we felt a new imperative to be Christ's ministers to the world's hurting people, whatever their hurts might be.

People don't want, or need, to be brow-beaten for their sins and shortcomings. They need, instead, that inner healing which empowers them to deal creatively with those sins and shortcomings.

So it is that Henri Nouwen tells us not to start with the issues which trouble us, but with God! He tells us that only as we become spiritually clear-headed, through the leading of the Spirit, can we deal successfully with such issues.

It is in this light that the invitation to do spiritual reading and study is offered as the road to that inner sense of God's presence of which the psalmist speaks when he says: "Everyday, when I take my life into my hands (to do whatever the day requires of me), I never forget thy instruction" (or thy presence). And there is power for living in that! For is that not what Jesus means when he says concerning our living: "Set your minds on the kingdom of heaven, above all else, and whatever else you need will come to you."

On Being Held Safe

Psalm 73:1-17; 1 Corinthians 12:12-14, 26 (RSV); Matthew 26:36-40

All of the spiritual disciplines we've been talking about, disciplines meant to enable us to learn to live as God's beloved, all of those disciplines are private. They are things we can only do for ourselves. Prayer-thoughts, through which we seek God's guidance and approval for our thoughts and activities; censoring what we allow into our consciousness in order to avoid inner clutter; finding meaning in the routines of our living; developing clarity of mind in our understanding of the gospel — all of these disciplines are, basically, private. To be sure, we can talk to one another about them. We can compare our various approaches to them. We may even offer suggestions as to what we have found to work for us. But, in the end, spiritual disciplines are private disciplines. No one can do them for us!

Having said that, we now need to be reminded that biblical religion is centered in community. In the Old Testament it is centered in the community called Israel. In the New Testament it is centered in the community called *church*. It is precisely that biblical fact which has led theologians over the ages to declare the impossibility of being truly Christian apart from the church.

Now that is not meant to be a threatening or a punishing statement. It is simply meant to say that we need community, both for the nurturing, and for the expression of our religious life. We need a place in which to *be held safe*. We need that kind of place described by St. Paul in the epistle lesson. He writes that the church is a place where "if one member suffers, all the members suffer with him or her; a place where, if one member is honored, all the members rejoice with him or her."

That's what I want to talk about in this sermon. I want to talk about the church as *a place for you* — as a place where you can be *held safe*.

I

The popularity of support groups, of course, attests to that need. If you look at the weekly newspaper calendar you will find support groups listed for any and all sorts of human conditions: grief, divorce, chronic illness, the permanent alteration of one's body through radical surgery, alcoholism, drug addiction, or the loss of a job. You name it and there's a support group for it.

Does that suggest to you, as it does to some, that people who go to such groups are weak? Not at all! They are simply those who are wise enough to realize that they need a place where they can be held safe, a place where they can be accepted, understood, taught, encouraged, and sent out again to get on with their living.

That's what the church is supposed to be. When Evangelical Church adopted as the motto, for both its evangelism program and the approach to its congregational life, the words, "Evangelical Church: A Place For You," these are precisely the things we had in mind. It is our intention to share the suffering of those who suffer, and to share the joy of those who rejoice. It is our intention to be a spiritual support group for all who come here. It is our hope to lead them to the knowledge that they are God's beloved, that there are programs here which can enable them to grow in that consciousness and way of life, and that we are here to support them in their spiritual journey. We need one another!

Years ago, when we got our first house with a fireplace in it, my wife and I were anxious to have a fire right away. Unfortunately, all I could scare up was a single log, a few sticks of kindling wood, and some paper. But I was determined! Beyond that, I didn't know you couldn't build a fire that way. Well, you can imagine the kind of fire we had! No sooner had the paper and kindling burned themselves out than the fireplace became, once again, a dark hole in the wall. Logs need other logs to burn against or they go out.

I forgot about that incident, which, incidentally, was one more illustration of why I flunked Boy Scouts. I forgot all about it until many years later when the need for logs to have other logs to burn against turned up in our confirmation curriculum as an illustration of the importance of the church community for a lively, *hot* faith.

We need the church! We need her preaching and teaching. We need her prayers and hymns. We need her sacraments for our spiritual nourishment and enlightenment.

But we also need her people! We need a place where we can be held safe against the storms of life. We need a place where we can experience the reality of God through loving, caring, warm-hearted human beings. We need to learn, through the ministry of the Body of Christ, that we are, indeed, God's beloved!

So it is that while today's psalm describes the spiritual confusion, and the disillusionment of one who tried to stay faithful in the face of the corruption which afflicted his society, and in the face of the apparent success of the crooks, the shysters, and the secularists — while the Psalmist describes his spiritual confusion and disillusionment in the face of all of that — he did not quit! He resolved his dilemma as he had been taught from a young age on as a member of that faith-community called Israel. He says:

> I tried to figure it out (all by myself) but I couldn't make any sense of it until I went into the sanctuary of God — into the congregation of God's faithful — then I understood what their end would be!

Henri Nouwen observes, at this point, that we cannot help but slip if we try to live as God's beloved *without accompaniment* — without someone to hold us, without some group to support us, without someone to respond to our needs by suggesting that we read this, pray about that, go here or go there, do this or do that, in order to find the answer to our questions and needs.

"Therefore," says Father Nouwen, "find a spiritual director! Find someone of spiritual depth and insight whose leading you can trust and let them be your spiritual mentor. And don't complain that you don't have anybody. God doesn't leave us alone!"

II

At this point I want to say a special word to the men and the boys among us. It is true that women and girls are much more realistic, much more honest, concerning their needs for intimacy and support than we are. They know their need for special women friends in whom they can find emotional nourishment, support, and direction.

By way of contrast, it is statistically confirmed that men seldom make such friends. We, in our rugged individualism and our macho image of maleness, try to *go it alone*.

Perhaps the reason John Bly — called "Iron John" — has achieved such popularity with his "Weekends For Men," in which men are led to get in touch with their inner-selves, is indicative of our need for a place of safety where we can experience our own sense of being God's beloved through the friendship and acceptance of other men. By some accounts, as many as 50,000 men of all ages have signed up for these weekends with John Bly.

Now those of you who are acquainted with descriptions of John Bly's approach may think him to be a bit weird. Maybe he is! Yet the sale of 27,000 copies of his videocassette, *A Gathering of Men*, and the sale of more than 10,000 transcripts of his appearance on Bill Moyer's PBS show illustrate the need of men for what others call a guru, and what Henri Nouwen calls a Spiritual Director.

Man or woman, girl or boy, we all need a place beyond spouse, beyond our family, where we can be *held safe* — a place where we can experience, in our inner-self, what it means to be God's beloved through the love, the caring, the wisdom, the insight and the instruction of a person, or persons, we can trust and respect.

That is what the church is meant to provide. That is why God called the church into being as a community in which our joys are heightened, our wounds are bound up, and our pilgrimage as God's beloved is enhanced; a place in which we can be *held safe*.

Finding Your True Self

Isaiah 55:1-5; Philippians 2:5-11 (RSV); Matthew 20:17-19; 21:1-11

To The Confirmation Class:

As you know, during these Sundays in Lent we have been talking about spiritual disciplines. We have been talking about prayer-thoughts by which we ask God whether what we are thinking and doing is right. We have mentioned the need to censor what we read, and what we watch on television, because much of it clutters up our thoughts and feelings with stuff that is really not good for us. We have talked about finding ways of serving God in the ordinary routines we do each day. And, of course, we have talked about the importance of church life and the study of the Bible and other Christian teachings to help us have a clear head whereby we may live as God's beloved people.

Now I want to talk about the purpose of all of this. I want to talk about God's call to you, and to me, to be a blessing to other people, to be God's ministers in the world.

I

In the reading from Isaiah, we heard the Prophet say that if we follow the ways of God we will enjoy God's love, and we will enjoy a rich, full life.

More than that, Isaiah tells us that even those who do not know God will come to God through us, through our ministry, because they will see God in us. Isn't that an awesome thought!

As you remember, after the Great Prayer of Thanksgiving in the Eucharist, we say together the Prayer of Oblation. In that prayer we offer ourselves to God as his obedient servants, thanking him that he has called us to be a Royal Priesthood.

In praying that prayer we remind ourselves that God calls us to be his ministers in the world, and that he gives us the power to do his work. Further, we say that prayer to remind ourselves of St. Paul's teaching, as we heard it in the reading from Philippians, that we are to be imitators of Jesus Christ. We are to have his mind and spirit in us. We are to be God's servants just as he was.

That, too, is what the Rite of Confirmation is all about! It most certainly is not your graduation out of the church, a sign that you have completed all of the class work we did together over the past seven months. No! Today you promise God that you will try to serve him as best you are able. You promise that you will find a way to be his ministers in whatever way you can in your life. And, in turn, I will put my hand on your head, as God's representative, and say the blessing which God offers you on this holy day in your life. Together we will pray that you will be able to live as God's beloved sons and daughters wherever you may go, and in whatever you may do.

II

But now I want to tell you a secret! You will get more out of being a minister for God than you will ever give. Jesus said it this way: "Whoever gives his life for my sake will find his/her true self."

Henri Nouwen, about whom you've heard me speak these past weeks, put it this way: "Whoever comes to you for help comes also as your teacher; they come as angels in disguise to bring you closer to God."

That means that sharing our faith with people who need our help not only helps them. It also helps us! It brings us closer to Jesus because we are doing just what he would do. It blesses us at the same time we are trying to be a blessing to others!

As I come closer to the time of retirement I find myself wondering just how faithful I have been as a minister of Jesus Christ. Have I truly made my life an oblation, a self-offering to God, or have I just done my job?

Well, I guess that question will only be answered for me on judgment day. But this much I do know. God has blessed me richly in my work. The people I have helped turned out to be his angels in disguise, bringing me closer to God. Let me give you two examples.

Last winter I met a young man whom I confirmed more than 20 years ago. He had come back for his grandfather's funeral. After the service he came to me and said: "I want to tell you something. When I was in your class you told me that I had a nice way of putting things, that I would be good with people. I've never forgotten that." Today he is a successful physician in family practice. Did my words lead him in that direction, or, at least, do they influence how he handles his patients? Either way, I was blessed by his words to me and encouraged in my ministry.

The second example: During the Christmas season I received a card and a note from a man I haven't heard from in years. He is now a 50-year-old retired naval officer in California, where he has resumed his great talent as an artist. When I knew Doug he was just a teenager in my first parish: a talented, nice kid from a broken home who *found himself* through life in the church. At any rate, he wrote to tell me that his mother had died. She was a lovely woman, whom I remember well. I suspect it helped him, now in his grief, to share the news with someone out of his youth who had been close to him back then. In the note he simply said that I had been an important part of his life as a teenager and that he wanted me to know now about his mom. Of course, I wrote to him at once.

Could it be that through these contacts from people to whom I ministered in the past I was hearing two of God's angels, in disguise, encouraging me and approving my ministry?

Ministry, either by clergy or lay people, is not just helping others. It is also being helped in the very process of being helpful. For in our doing for others we are brought close to God. We are converted, and reconverted, to the Christ-centered life, making our own trip to Jerusalem, so to speak, in order that we, like Jesus, might be found faithful.

All of which is to say that it is in putting ourselves second, so that God can use us for his purpose in the world, that we find our true selves: our purpose in life, our true happiness.

III

So let me end by saying that you are being confirmed, not because you know what Christians believe. You are being confirmed, not because you think the church has some neat programs you might like to try. You are being confirmed, not even because you think you may want to help other people. No! You are being confirmed because God has called you to have the same mind and the same spirit in you that Jesus had: that mind and spirit, that inner sense that God calls you to be his servants; to be his Royal Priesthood; to be his chosen workers. God wants you to be a blessing to others so that you might also be blessed by discovering your true self, your true purpose in life.

So let your prayer this day be those deeply moving lines of St. Francis of Assisi as he prayed:

> *Lord, make me an instrument of thy peace. Where there is hatred let me sow love; where there is injury, pardon; where there is doubt, faith; where there is despair, hope; where there is darkness, light; and where there is sadness, joy. O Divine Master, grant that I may not so much seek to be consoled as console; to be understood as to understand; to be loved as to love. For it is in giving that we receive; it is in pardoning that we are pardoned; it is in dying that we are born to eternal life.*

Rising To New Life

Daniel 12:1-3; 2 Corinthians 5:15-18a; Luke 23:50—24:16

Isn't it phenomenal? Even Jesus' closest friends and associates didn't believe his resurrection!

But then I think you will agree that many of us, if really pressed to state our Easter beliefs, would also express doubts about the resurrection story. For we find it easier to accept the idea of immortality, taught by Greek philosophy, than to accept resurrection. It's easier to believe that a little piece of us, that piece the Greeks called *soul*, never dies. It's easier to believe in the immortality of the soul than to believe in the totality of death and, after that, resurrection to new life.

Nevertheless, the gospel speaks of death in all its awesome completeness. It reports that our Lord died, that he was entombed, and that the women were making preparation to embalm his body in order to prevent the putrefaction of his flesh. The historic creeds of the church affirm the same thing: "He was crucified, dead and buried!"

In like manner, the reading from Daniel, the earliest teaching on resurrection, speaks of those "who sleep in the dust of the earth." It speaks of those who sleep the sleep of death!

All of which is to say that the scriptures offer us no hope of immortality in the Greek sense of having an indestructible soul. When we die, we die! And if we have any hope at all for eternity, it is through the power of a gracious, loving God, powerful enough to bring even the dead to life. That is the Christian understanding of eternal life. It is God's gift. It is not a part of our basic nature.

II

That is why we need to anchor our lives, not in pagan philosophy or in that sentimental view of existence which creates its own delusions of immortality, but in the power of God to create new life even out of death.

Henry Nouwen offers a story which helps us understand the true nature of the Easter promise:

> *In Holland, during a yearly peace march in which 3,000 high school students walk and talk together for three days, the leaders were startled by the sentimentality that characterized the interaction between the marchers. For these usually quite reserved Dutchmen, holding hands was the most important experience, and the hour of farewell saw a railway station filled with hugging and crying boys and girls. In their reflection after the march, some marchers wondered how they could ever live happily again after such an experience of communion. While feeling distant from the religious words and gestures of the church which had called them to march, their unique experience of togetherness stirred up powerful and frightening sentiments.*[1]

We all know the power of such experiences. I hope today's Easter liturgy will be one such experience for you. Flowers, music, pageantry, together with a promise concerning that most profound of all of life's questions, "What's next?" touch our hearts and emotions. It uplifts us! It thrills us! It imbues us with new spiritual certainty!

But soon the service will end, and how, then, do we sustain such emotions and sentiments? The answer is: "We do not!"

Father Nouwen is right, at this point, when he reminds us that sentimentality, whether rooted in worship or in group solidarity and endeavor, is never enough! For when it comes to the ultimate questions of life and death, more is demanded than you and I can, ultimately, create through our own endeavors. Only God can deal with such questions.

And that is the heart of the Easter Gospel. Today's celebration is a testimony to the power of God to bring new life even out of death; and that is not a sentimental wish. It is not a philosophical hope, born of human grief, while standing at the graveside of lost loved ones. The Easter hope of new life is an affirmation of faith centered in the story of the empty tomb, in the story of our Lord's walk with the two disciples on the Emmaus road, even though they didn't then recognize him, and confirmed in his continual presence with us in Word and Sacrament.

This, says Henri Nouwen, is what we express when we take bread and wine in thanksgiving:

> *We do not eat the bread to still our hunger, or drink wine to quench our thirst. We.... eat and drink.... in the realization that God's presence is (found in) the presence of the One who came, but who is still to come; who touched our hearts, but who has not yet taken all our sadness away. And so when we share some bread and some wine together, we do this not as people who have arrived, but as people who can support each other in patient expectation until we see him again. And then our hearts will be full of joy, a joy that no one can take away from us.*[2]

I like those words because they are so realistic! They are realistic in that they state something that all thinking Christians know by experience, namely, that we live in the interim. We live between our Lord's Resurrection and his return. We live between the fulfillment of God's promises of a recreated world and the world as we know it. We live between heaven's invitation to hope and to work for something better, and the world's invitation to join its skepticism and despair; and skepticism and despair are quite a temptation, given the *clay feet* of the world's leaders, in the face of which our citizens talk about choosing the lesser of evils as they *size up* candidates during election campaigns.

III

Which leads me to say a word about the new life which the gospel offers, not only as a post-death experience, but also as something to be experienced in this life.

In the reading from 2 Corinthians, St. Paul writes: "When anyone is united to Christ he is a new creation."

It was Dr. Eric Berne, the eminent psychiatrist, who developed *Transactional Analysis* as a means of therapy, who said: "We are born princes. It is the civilizing process which turns us into frogs!"

Biblically speaking, we were created in God's likeness. That means we were created with all of the potential and nobility known to the human race. Unfortunately, it is the sinful perversion of that potential, and of that intended nobility, through a misuse of our freedom, knowledge, and power, that we become frogs rather than the princes and princesses to which Genesis points.

In other words, sin, in both its personal and its socially debilitating forms, is not simply wickedness. Sin is the unashamed compromising of our basic potential as God's beloved. To make matters worse, included in that compromise is the sin of those people whose behavior leads to the downfall of others. Elected officials who betray the public trust and create a cynical and resentful citizenry; businesses which bilk the public, including their own employees; employees who withhold an honest day's work; a socio-economic system which exalts some while it holds others in subjection; parents who are too busy to attend to the emotional and spiritual needs of their children; children who are without respect, and without a sense of responsibility toward their parents: all of these things, and more, are part of the social process which Dr. Berne describes as creating frogs out of us human beings, who, by God's design, were intended to be the princes and princesses of his world.

It is against that background that St. Paul calls for your conversion and mine. He invites us to become *one in spirit* with the Risen Lord, that we may become Christ's new creation; that we may find in this life the new life to which Easter points.

That's what it means to live as God's beloved through those spiritual discipines of which we have previously spoken.

IV

And now a poetic conclusion to our thoughts about the new life to which the Easter gospel invites us:

The Crowning Wonder

...They saw him die the malefactor's death,
They saw his body sealed within the tomb,
They saw the guard that watched it night and day.
But His true self was not to bind nor hold,
And three days later, as He had foretold,
He came again among them as of old, —
Came in His own marred body, bearing still
The ragged nail-wounds in His hands and feet, —
Came in the flesh, and ate and drank with them;
And not of them alone was He thus seen,
But unto many who had known Him well.
Unto His own, he spoke full lovingly,
And pledged them all anew to do His will,
Till all [folk] everywhere should know
God's love for [them],
And His eternal longing for [their] good.
No [one] may see the face of God and live;
His Love enfolds us like the air and light;
His wonders are about us everywhere;
But finite cannot grasp the infinite
And so He veiled His Godhead in the flesh
That all might see and know Him in His son, —
Might see in Him the fullness of His love
And share with Him the victory He won...[3]

To which I would add that for God's beloved, who are already a new creation in Christ, for them, for us, when the body is done — ashes to ashes, dust to dust — for us God steps in and the new life already begun in Christ goes on to that fulfillment we call eternity.

---

1. Used by permission of Henri Nouwen.

2. Excerpt from *Out Of Solitude* by Henri J. M. Nouwen, Copyright 1974 by Ave Maria Press, Notre Dame, IN 46556. All rights reserved. Used with permission of the publisher.

3. John Oxenham, Excerpt from "The Crowning Wonder," *The Story Of Jesus In The World's Literature*, ed. Edward Wagenknecht, Creative Age Press, Inc., New York, 1946, p. 451.